Bless It All Baby !

♡ ☮ ☺

Bridgit

Advise & Consent

Simple Soul Wisdom

LovePeaceJoy, LLC
PO Box 96 Mason, MI 48854
www.lovepeacejoy.net
Published 2006

Advise & Consent
By Bridget Bernadette
Copyright 2006

ISBN 0-9768815-0-0

Quote from CONVERSATIONS WITH GOD by Neale Donald Walsch, copyright (c) 1995 by Neale Donald Walsch. Used by permission of G.P. Putnam's Sons, a division of Penguin Group (USA) Inc.

Cover Design: Bridget Bernadette & Rick Hoffmeyer

Photos of author: Rick Hoffmeyer / Cover
                   Allison Sunshine Marion / About The Author

Printed in the United States of America

Advise & Consent
Simple Soul Wisdom

An Inspirational Bouquet

Written & Photographed By
Bridget Bernadette

Dedicated In Loving Memory
Of My Father:

You are always with me.
Your love lives.
You are not lost, but gone before.

Acknowledgements

My gratitude extends to the extensive network of support
that God provides me with in this lifetime. My love pours out to my
family, friends, neighbors, co-workers, clients and acquaintances:
A heart filled thank-you to each and every one of you;
all of you make this book possible.

Honorable mention goes to my husband and children,
Rick, Olivia Jane and Alex.
They live with me, they love me and they forgive me.
I am so blessed.

Another life anchoring accomplice, my Anne.
Anne Marie DeMarco, my best friend and editor.
Thanks for never, ever giving up on me.

Although the list could go on...
Special recognition for assisting with the birth of this book:
Hannah Colegrove, Kristine McNease, Rita Schoettle, Sharon Bennett,
Vandorn Hinnant, Katrina VanHuss, Richard Baldwin, Jamie Robinson,
Eileen Droscha, Margaret Doolittle & Mary Elaine Kiener, RN, PhD
Bless You All!

Sharon Bennett, CEO & Founder
Premier Pet Products
PREMIER.COM

Foreword
By Sharon Bennett

Despite all my maneuvering I am stuck. I missed my morning flight for an important business meeting. At least a dozen frantic phone calls, and still no other airline can get me there on time, so I grudgingly resign myself to the last seat on a later flight. It's my own fault, really. Stayed up too late last night, didn't double check my itinerary.

Even worse is that gnawing, all-too-familiar guilt... my stop in Detroit had been "personal"... true, it had been scheduled mostly in pursuit of spiritual clarity, but it was also an indulgence, with the hope of longings to be fulfilled... and my religious heritage is quite clear that such desire is wrong. And now I am certain that God is showing me His displeasure in a practical and most obvious manner.

As I finally board the flight and make my way to seat 19B, I have no idea just how clear a Message is about to be sent to me.

Before the plane even takes off, exhaustion wins out. I wake up about an hour later, and notice the woman next to me reading a book, "***Conversations With God.***" I am curious and ask her about it. She says she is going to the "Celebrate Your Life" Conference, and on the way she reads the book by one of the featured speakers, Neale Donald Walsch.

This is what the back jacket said:

I have heard the crying of your heart. I have seen the searching of your soul. I know how deeply you have desired the Truth. In pain you called out for it, and in joy. Unendingly have you beseeched Me. Show Myself. Explain Myself. Reveal Myself.

I am doing so here, in terms so plain, you cannot misunderstand. In language so simple, you cannot be confused. In vocabulary so common, you cannot get lost in the verbiage.

So go ahead now. Ask Me anything. Anything. I will contrive to bring you the answer. The whole universe will I use to do this. So be on the lookout; this book is far from My only tool. You may ask a question, then put this book down. But watch.

Listen.

The words to the next song you hear. The information in the next article you read. The story line of the next movie you watch. The chance utterance of the next person you meet. Or the whisper of the next river, the next ocean, the next breeze that caresses your ear - all these devices are Mine; all these avenues are open to Me. I will speak to you if you will listen. I will come to you if you will invite Me. I will show you then that I have always been there.

All Ways   **Conversations With God** *By Neale Donald Walsch*

Without hesitation, and with free-flowing tears, I begin to pour out my life story to this total stranger next to me. The struggle of my spiritual journey finds a listening ear and a shoulder to cry on. And then this amazing woman who embodies grace and inner beauty, begins to share a bit about her own journey, her perceptions about the love and the peace and the joy of the Spirit Of Life.

Then, Bridget Bernadette (for she is the instrument God has chosen to use this day) reaches inside her briefcase and pulls out a small spiral bound book. She seems ever so slightly hesitant. She whispers that I am the first person, beyond her family, to view the contents of her book. Bridget then says, "Spirit voices that you need to read this."

And I do, then and there, cover to cover.

And the words of the very first poem, *"Black and White,"* fall like sweet, heavy drops of rain on a barren and broken heart. I drink in the love and the wisdom of the Spirit speaking Life to my soul.

Those moments, and the "Simple Soul Wisdom" of ***Advise & Consent,*** gave birth to a new understanding and vision and hope. Almost immediately that "guilt," my former constant companion, began to melt away with this new dawning Light. The eyes of my heart began to open and embrace the path that is mine: to discover and to breathe in the true Love of the Spirit, and then to learn to walk out this Love for myself and for others... Love that is reflected in a rainbow of color, not the black and white prison of my past.

I believe that, for me, the journey IS the destination. And the pages of this profound little book serve as a compass, a map, a light on the pathway. There are no "accidents". This treasure found its way to you, too, for a Reason. May you find the freedom of love, peace and joy on the journey that is yours alone, and all of ours together.

Contents

Life Is Not All Black & White

Life requires living in color,
lifting the shadows and sparking the vibrancy
of the moment at hand.

Every experience I live brings me to this conclusion.
The most explicit way of explaining this philosophy...

It stems from the day my soul arose from a somber sleep.

Magically, my senses woke up:
I visualize beauty and goodness everywhere,
I hear the swift, uplifting flow of music in my heart,
I deeply inhale the scents that soothe the soul,
I taste the sweetness of every moment,
I feel the transcendence of energy through my being.

I now realize the gray between the black & white
renders the rainbow of hope!

I am in the most beautiful state.
I love myself.
I can not help but love
everything else.

The Beholder

NOW

It may be the first,
perhaps the last;

Just do it now
or else this time will pass.

Prioritize

Decide...
      what must be done.

Then Do It.
The Rest Will Wait.

Know this works
      and is necessary to survive
            every moment of this life.

Fear Not
An Unknown
Future.

Mercy Falls
In Believing.

For Lessons
Unfold,
Gracefully,
Perfectly,
As
We Choose
And
God Intends.

To The Right

Body Language

Says everything without a word.
Stand up straight.
Look forward.
Keep your eyes focused.
Stay in alignment with your heart.
Plant your feet on the ground.
Listen to your body talk.
Speak.

One Step Forward
Two Steps
Back...

In Kindergarten
you learn to
name your emotions.

As an adult
you are taught to
ignore them.

Escape, return to what you know.

Regress.

Boundaries...

Form With Loving Discipline.

House Rules

The issue is not winning or losing.
The importance lies in playing the game
with goodwill and ample effort.

Knowing you did your best,
that you support a cause you whole-heartedly believe in.

Passion and Love precede outcome
with these House Rules...
Everyone wins.

Too sweet
too simple
too kind
to be
anything
other than
a friend
to
me.

FRIEND

The Beauty

The beauty bestowed in a woman
is relevant to
her capacity to endure
much
and not show it.

Will I die
for my beliefs
rather than
concede to
what I feel?

This Concerns Me

Senses

I need to trust
my senses.
They shower me with truth.
What I feel...
Of course it exists!
How dare I deny what I know
to be true.

Tired of cleaning up messes,
After the damage is done,
I choose to be proactive.

Reach Out And Halt The Nonsense

My Favorite Part...

The moment when you
close the door,
cut the crap and communicate.

When you connect.

Let Every Loss
Be A Gain.
Then
Balance May Be
Obtained.

On One Foot

Next,

Do not dread a single minute.
Have faith that every experience
leads you to the next.
That, in itself,
is indeed a good thing.

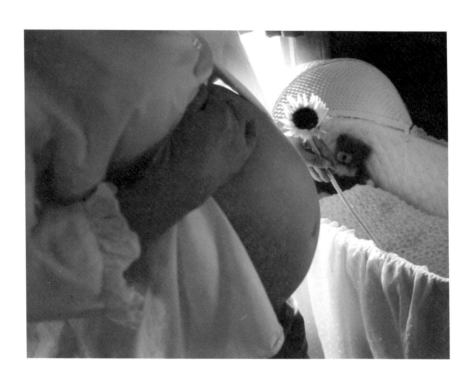

If I believe in one thing...

                    Timing is it.

Without the perfectly executed moment...

                            Life itself be lost.

                                   Conception

I Love You Because...

I love you
because...
you are a beautiful soul.
I love you
because...
you love me back.
I love you
because...
I have no doubt
this is the way it should be.

Family

Forgive Them
For Being Who They Are.
Forgive Yourself
For Judging Them.
Forgive.

Marvel Unconditional Love.

It is of the normal natural
progression that women take
after their mothers.

Heredity cannot be lost,
forgotten or tucked away
in a back pocket.

Some things carry on...

No Matter What

Advice

Tell your truth
as you know it.

Bare your naked soul and
hide in fear no more.
State what weighs heavy
on your mind.

Express what you feel.

Everything
comes with something...

Fact

Stomach It

Sometimes I notice too much lies on my plate
and I simply cannot stomach it all in one setting.

Privileges
wear a pricetag.

Nothing
is
free.

My Thoughts Exactly...

The only reason
I'll let you go
is to support
you in another way.

Only

Of course my observations
remain subjective
in the most objective manner.

Perceptions

S.T.O.P.

Stop - Think - Observe - Pray
Give life order.
Pick up the mess
that surrounds you.

THEN LOOK.

What do you see?

Define your life with
thought & character.
Stop - Think - Observe - Pray

S.T.O.P.

Shhh...

Turn away, do not look...
unless you are ready to see the truth.

You cannot lie to yourself with anything but ignorance.
Once you know, it's over.

Knowing changes everything.

A Calling

Wake Up!

Listen Closely.
Dreams Speak To You.

Create Life With Heart's Desire.

Believe The Calling Of
Divine Intervention.

Move The World With Will.

Wake Up!

Catch Me...

My Falling Faith
Surrenders
Control.

What Goes Around...

Like a child plays,
I simply love
what I am doing
and
I do it just because...
I love it.
Love motivates me
and
true to heart I give my all.

I take time
to love
all
that I encounter.

I view life
so beautifully,
one frame at a time.

Snapshots

Splendid

I feel
like a child
who just learned how to read:

The world is
mine!

One Day

It is amazing, breath taking...
when relationships
transcend and rise above our expectations.

One day it simply is.

Humanness

There are good people everywhere.

Although, few possess the
                    patience of a saint,
                        wisdom of a healer,
                            or powers of God.

So, the rest of us learn along the way.

Our humanness shows.

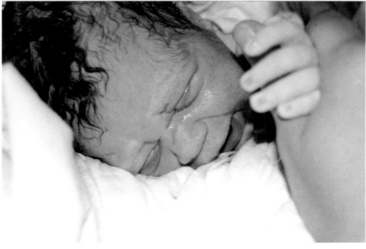

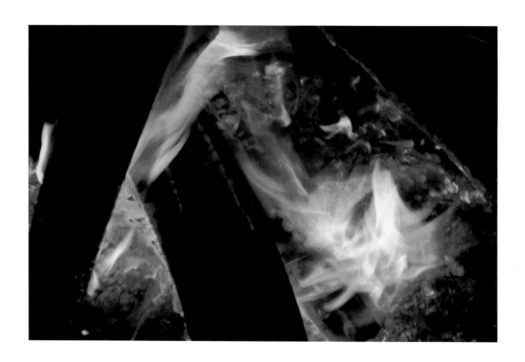

Take It Easy

That is like asking me
not to breathe.

Afraid?

I am not afraid
of death...
I hold her hand,
she comforts me.

I am afraid of
not living...

I don't bite, at least not too often,
and when I do bite it's not very hard.
I simply provide enough umph
to leave an impression.

Making Marks

Plug In & Connect;
Do Not Drain Your Soul.
Love It...
Protect It...
Respect It...

Your Soul Nourishes & Guides You
Through This Life.

Learn

When you PRAY,
TRUST the answer,
for you ask GOD to intervene.

Okay...
Remind Me To Watch My Words

life

i like the game
i define
i make the rules
i decide
i choose

what's your game?

Like Every Other Day

I change today.
Just like every other day.

I am a constant butterfly!

Always
clean your wounds
before you
cover them up.

Words Of Wisdom

Sleep Well

Life changes.
Do not be sorry,
it is just the way things are.
The contrast
between yesterday and today
and the way things will be tomorrow
generates apprehension
for being
Here & Now.
So, in this moment of illumination:
PRAY
in the light of knowing
all is well.
Rest your head and pause the commotion.
Succumb to peace of mind
beyond the business of control.
Close your eyes my child;
sleep well tonight,
sleep well.

Gratitude...

Immeasurable gratitude spills forth as I complete these pages! I gave birth to the baby, but the child is indisputably ours...

Love, Love, Love to you all!

Thank you, **Rick Hoffmeyer**, my loving and devoted husband of twenty years. Without you, my words and photos may still be sitting on a shelf! Your constant technical support, along with your spirited motivation, guides me through this process.

Dearest **Mary Elaine Kiener, RN, PhD**, thank you for the title! Your beauty and kindness shines upon my being and your wisdom resonates with my soul!

For nurturing and growing the remarkable "*Laughing Flower*" on the front cover, thank you, **Dar Marcusse and Greg Smith**. And bless you for watering me with your love.

God winked the day we met, **Rita Schoettle**! Our spirits unite with divine recognition. We groove together. Your phenomenal gift of sharing spiritual insight with love, laughter and good intent sets a fine example. You bring peace into the hearts of so many... The world is a better place because of you.

Sharon Bennett, synchronicity bridges our beginning. As instruments of God, we continue to support each other through this journey with unconditional love. You are an earth angel. Your entrepreneurial guidance spreads its wings, so I may soar!

To the woman who orchestrates the financial management of LovePeaceJoy, LLC, **Barbara Plecas**, I would be lost without you! Your mastery of accounting only accentuates the many talents you possess. You share your light and love so generously.

Jane Buckle, PhD, RN, your brilliance shines! You cast rainbows of hope through researching and teaching. Your philosophy of putting the "care" back into our "health care system" motivates me always.

Once again, **Jane Rosemont**, you magically appear to inspire me. Your astounding talent to paint color into life amazes me, always. Your vibrant energy and creative soul continually expands; you live life so magnificently.

Celebrating your teachings to the world, **Margaret Doolittle**, I salute you. With awe, admiration and the deepest of respect, I honor you and bestow my gratitude!

Dearest **Vandorn**, for all the LOVE! The vibration of LOVE which unites all, merges our souls and the exuberant exhileration escalates the LOVE... It's all about LOVE!

To my soul sister, **Kristine McNease**...the orange crayon is yours! Continue brightening up the lives of all who are blessed to know your loving self. Keep laughing, loving and living well.

To the woman whose angelic voice and wise soul leads me to believe in the beauty of my heart's desire, **Hannah Colegrove,** may all your dreams come true.

Katrina VanHuss, the "process" drew us together; we were kindred spirits destined to unite. Your marketing expertise in the launching of Advise & Consent, be as essential as your friendship is to my heart and soul! You, my friend, are priceless.

And thank you, **Rich Baldwin,** for sharing your wisdom with a kind, jovial and generous nature. Scripted and poetic be the union of our souls. God's mystery unfolds...

Extraordinary exemplifies your nature, **Jamie Robinson**. You serve community whole-heartedly. For your dedication and willingness to give I applaud you!

Eileen Droscha, my vivacious local librarian and dear friend. What a gift you offer; you provide endless opportunities for learning! We share the passion to serve...

For all the JOY, I thank you **Sean, Janice, Katelynn, Kyle and Lawrence O'Boyle**! The depth of my gratitude knows no boundaries. Years of love bind us into the fabric of one another. Forever our souls shall know the essence of the other.

And always to **Anne Marie DeMarco**, for showing up week after week and year after year. You ROCK! You are my hero! A tried and true friend. My great big heart runneth over with gratitude. I love you so much!

Heartfelt Appreciation To All
Photographed Individuals:

Lawrence O'Boyle, Rick Hoffmeyer, Linda Stephan (Mom), Zachary John Joseph Stephan, Olivia Jane Hoffmeyer, Janice O'Boyle, Katy Stephan, Allison Sunshine Marion, Katelynn O'Boyle, DeLany McFate, Rosaline Kuiper, Danten McFate, Anna Stephan, Kyle Marion, Conner Marion, Cameron Marion, Kaleb Marion, Alex Hoffmeyer, Danielle Stephan, Robyn Kihn, Kasey Kihn, Michael J Hoffmeyer, Fran Hoffmeyer, Pastor Roy Schroeder, Raymond Ruechert Jr. (RJ), Dr. Kwabena Appiah, Tyler Arnett, Madison Nodus-Rydal, Melissa Loszewski, Gary Marion and Sharon Bennett.

Thank you for letting your souls shine.

Photo By: Sunshine

About The Author

Bridget Bernadette speaks straight from the heart with her words and images. Through her many labors of love (both personal and professional), she reveals astute observations that inspire the soul. It is these simple truths that shine. She passionately shares this knowledge by opening eyes and awakening hearts to soulful living.

While nursing souls to their optimal state of being, she discovers depths of wisdom through serving others. So, with a strong foundation in traditional medicine, she chooses to expand her practice with complementary therapies in order to holistically facilitate healing. Treating mind, body, spirit and soul, Bridget enters relationships with a listening ear, keen vision and an intuitive sense, with a focus on spirituality and health. This integrative approach offers hope, comfort and options...

Advocating for souls begins at home for Bridget, as a wife, mother, friend and neighbor. She deeply believes in family, community and loving all that you do. It is the balancing of these roles that acts as a catalyst to her bathtub writings. After a long day, whether tending to the children, working at the bedside of a patient or volunteering her services, finding twenty minutes to soak in the events of the day and let out all the emotion becomes her secret to sanity. All of Bridget's books begin in the bathtub!